The Tao is hidden and without name.
The Tao alone nourishes and brings everything to fulfilment.

L A O   T S U

Tao Te Ching*

The Path

To Thyself

IVAN STANCHEV

KIBEA

KIBEA'S BOOK & HEALTH CENTRE & RESTAURANT

Sofia 1000, Dr. G. Valkovich Street 2A

BOOKSHOP: tel. +359 2 988 01 93
HEALTH FOOD RESTAURANT: tel. +359 2 980 30 67

* Lao Tsu – Tao Te Ching, transl. by Gia-Fu Feng and Jane English, Wildwood House 1991, first published 1972.

Ivan Stanchev

THE PATH TO THYSELF

ISBN: 978–954–474–537–0

To my wife Rossy — for her love and kindness and for her boundless patience and to our son Stanislav (Stenly) — for his gift of music

Chapter one

If I speak in the tongues of men and of angels, but have not love, I am only a resounding gong or a clanging cymbal. If I have the gift of prophecy and can fathom all mysteries and all knowledge, and if I have a faith that can move mountains, but have not love, I am nothing. If I give all I possess to the poor and surrender my body to the flames, but have not love, I gain nothing.

1 CORINTHIANS, 13:1–3

eight

The Prince was celebrating his coming of age. The court was full of guests from near and far, for peace was the chief weapon that the old king used to expand his state and multiply his friends. The feast went on for three days. Delighted and fascinated, the guests talked about how the Prince had inherited his father's wisdom, and how he was certain to have a bright future.

Indeed, the Prince had mastered the martial arts to perfection. He was almost invariably the winner in sports contests, but his heart was more in the arts – he enjoyed studying the languages of distant peoples and listening to the discussions of philosophers and wise men. Sometimes he would even join in the discourse, and they would be astonished by the maturity of his thoughts.

It was a bright day in July. The sky was the colour of blue velvet. In the park, the fountains were singing in joy and spinning threads of sunshine. The grass was whispering softly, and squirrels were chasing each other in the trees.

The Prince was standing on a small pier under the giant silver willows by the lake, leaning on the rail and contemplating his reflection in the water. A strange anxiety filled his soul. "There it is again, this strange and irresistible impulse, this unbridled energy for something great in the future. What do I want, actually? This longing is perhaps the noblest part of me, but what should I do about it? Will it prove fruitful, or is it just a vain restlessness of the mind and a thrill of the heart?..."

nine

In the lake he could see the reflections of the trees, the greenery and the sky. The water was very still. It was deep, calm and wise, but silent.

Fluff was floating in the air, carrying all the warmth and effulgence of summer.

Perched on the top branch of a dead tree, a swallow was singing.

The Prince looked up and listened. The swallow was endlessly repeating its long warble, culminating each time in an exultant cadence overflowing with affection and happiness.

More swallows were singing in the distance, alone or in choirs, their heads turned to the sky and the sun.

"How happy this bird is for being a part of the beauty of this world," the Prince exclaimed. "In its tiny head, it seems to have some knowledge and understanding that are beyond my reach... Indeed, how it sings in praise of life!"

"Nonsense," said a frog that was squatting on a water lily's green leaf. She was trying hard to look wise and absorbed in thought, just like the water, but she could not resist the temptation to speak her mind. "Nothing in this world is forever! And besides, what sort of elocution is that? One can't make out a word. My own little frogs sing much more clearly! But then, you can't expect much from a creature that flies in the skies, can you? Ha-ha! Real safety is in the swamp," she scoffed, and flopped among the lilies.

She regarded herself as universally competent, and commented on anything and everything. She took a particular pride in her offspring. Small as they were, her children were so prudent!

The Prince spoke many languages, but the frogs' language he could not understand.

ten

He was watching the water lilies. Their white flowers danced on the water surface like palms cupped round a candle, and emitted a gentle golden light.

"Indeed," thought the Prince, "life is the most wonderful gift there is."

He fixed his gaze on the old tree. It was nearly stripped of its bark. Although it was dead, it still stood among the living trees, its trunk as white as a skeleton.

"They all grew from its seeds. It fulfilled its purpose. What would mine be?" the Prince mused. "Why does one struggle and suffer? Isn't human life as brief as a candle's flame? Do we indeed disappear without a trace in time? Or does life go on beyond death? This is what the scriptures say. But is it true? Could this be but a pious myth, a vain dream of eternal life, a consolation for the spiritually weak? Men are vulnerable and dependent! It is ridiculous to suppose that we were created in God's likeness... Yet, deep inside, I feel that each of us is a universe, each is different and unique. How can this be preserved through Eternity? This is the question, but where can I find the answer?"

At that point, a noisy bunch of boisterous people came out from the wood, with the Prince's younger brother in their lead.

"That's where you've been hiding!," he exclaimed.

"When you are young as the green leaves in May, solitude is a promise rather than pain," the court jester added thoughtfully.

The group swarmed around the Prince, and the loveliest of the maidens bowed deep before him. If he had not been so absorbed in thought, he could have noticed the deep light in her eyes.

She presented to him a red rose, and the jester blindfolded him with a piece of cloth.

eleven

"It's your turn," his brother cried out, "let's see who you'll catch!"

And off they went playing blind man's bluff. The Prince followed the laughter and the cries, trying to catch someone, but his heart was not in it and he only tagged the jester.

"I'm the fool in the game, too," the jester gibed. "What prize is a fool?"

"Still, to earn your release, answer me: what is it that can preserve man through Eternity?"

"It has never been closer to you. All you need are faster feet and a bit more agile hands than it takes to tag a jester."

"A riddle is no answer to a riddle."

"Better look into the eyes of the Little Princess who gave you the red flower. There you will find what you are looking for. Only love preserves life through Eternity."

"I thought you were wise, but you seem to be just witty," the Prince complained. "You are talking of love that can be good enough for the swallows, but there must be more to a man's life."

And he walked away, leaving the others to go on with their game.

Only the Little Princess ran away, the light in her eyes having turned into tears.

The Prince went to the sage and asked him the same question:

"What is it that can preserve man through Eternity?"

The sage replied:

"Only art can elevate the perishable and make it eternal. It catches the intransient like a bee that transforms the ephemeral blossom's nectar into honey. A prince, however, is not obliged to take up art; it suffices to understand art,

twelve

thirteen

which is a talent you possess. The Eternity of Rulers is called history. It is, indeed, an art to rule wisely and in peace."

"No, not for me. Power hardens the heart, and what is in me will remain unrealised. Something is welling up inside me, something that has to do with Eternity and the mystery of life. But where can I find the answer?"

"The mystery of life and Eternity belongs to God, son," the priest interrupted, having listened to the conversation. "Humble your heart, for the reckless search for knowledge is the original sin."

"Forgive me, father, but how can one live without resolving the mystery of life? Isn't this what the Scriptures are meant for? Explain to me, why are we supposed to atone for the original sin that took place at the dawn of time? Is it in guilt and suffering that we can find wisdom? Doesn't it reside in the joy of life?"

"Blasphemous words! I don't want to listen!" the priest shook his head sternly.

"If no one knows the meaning of the Scriptures any more, then no one can explain them so that people can understand them."

The priest did not answer. He turned his back and walked away. He had something more important to do: adjust the tiara on his head.

The Prince walked out onto the front terrace.

Below, he could see the roofs of homes and temples, the bridges and the river meandering around the steep hill where the palace stood in the center of the park. The sound of horseshoes and anvils had faded away as twilight approached.

Suddenly, the sound of strings broke the silence, followed by a song... It was like a call, like a longing for something wonderful but unreachable, noble and mournful.

fourteen

The Prince rushed down the steps and there, sitting beneath a tree, was a stranger with a white beard. He was playing his cittern and singing. The sandals on his bare feet were covered with dust. A boy was standing beside him, a small bowl in his hand. The Prince approached quietly, wishing that the song would never end... Beautiful moments are so short-lived, however!

"Who are you?"

"I am a singer," the stranger replied. "I travel the world to collect songs."

"Whose song were you playing?"

"It is a very old song. No one remembers who created it."

"This song moved me deeply. Teach me how to create music. It seems to me that music can transform a fleeting moment into eternity!"

"Your words are wise," the singer smiled, "but not every man can find music in his soul."

Being blind, he was not aware that he was talking to the Prince, hence he told him the truth.

"All right then. I can feel I can!"

"Stay with me for five years and you will find out whether music is your vocation."

"Five years!" the Prince exclaimed.

"You will test yourself during that time. It is, indeed, a short period. A true artist only creates a single song, the song of his own life,,, And it goes like this..."

Pensively, the stranger stroke a chord...

A small coin fell on the pavement with a clink. A fat noble looked out of a window. He didn't notice the Prince in the shadow of the tree, and shouted at the singer:

fifteen

"Hey, you there! You're not letting me sleep, and I have important state matters to handle tomorrow! Take the coin and get out of here!"

The Prince felt confused. The song resounded in him, and he longed to follow its call, but a doubt crept in his soul like a viper:

"The music evoked neither memories nor feelings in that man. Would it, then, be preserved through the centuries to come? It seems that noble souls are indeed rare..."

Without a word, he dropped a gold coin in the stranger's bowl and walked away, followed by the cittern's quiet moan.

Although his family would miss him, the following day the Prince saddled his horse, bid everyone farewell and left: he had decided to travel the world and find the answer to the question of what could preserve man through eternity.

The Little Princess went all the way to the town gate to see him off.

She looked sad as she unclasped the small ruby pendant she was wearing and put it in his hand.

"I have done nothing to deserve this," the Prince smiled. "I don't even know what lies ahead, and whether I will ever be able to return the kindness." To his own surprise, however, he leaned towards her.

"I am giving it to you so that it can protect you. I want nothing in return," the Little Princess replied quietly.

As she was pulling the amulet over his head, he chanced to look into her eyes and suddenly realised that it was like seeing her for the first time...

Before he could utter a word, however, she had walked away.

The Prince's gaze followed her until she disappeared in the crowd of people and carts.

sixteen

seventeen

eighteen

Having endured the long journey, the Prince arrived in a city made of white marble on the shore of a blue sea, surrounded by silvery olive groves. Behind fences lemons and pomegranates were ripening. Sculptures adorned the squares.

In a yard, the clank of a hammer could be heard. Someone was singing a sorrowful song, and it floated in the air like disconsolate mourning. Captivated by it, the Prince went in.

Inside, amidst marble blocks, sculpted columns and wooden scaffolds, a sculptor was working with his disciples. The Prince watched for a long time as a girl slowly emerged from the marble; her beauty could only be compared to that of the Little Princess. He recalled her hand: a giving hand. He cherished her gesture deep in his heart, like a fond secret.

Grabbing a hammer and a chisel, he started shaping that generous hand out of a piece of marble.

When he was done, he noticed that the sculptor was standing behind him. Sparkling beneath a massive forehead, his eyes had the power to unveil secrets hidden in stones.

"Stay with me," he offered. "In two years, your sculptures will be the embodiment of perfection."

The Prince's heart jumped in joy, and he uttered words of gratitude. Just then he caught a glimpse of a metal cast, the face of a woman from a strange race. Full of melancholy and mysterious thoughtfulness, the bronze features

nineteen

held such a perfect beauty that the Prince stood speechless for a very long time.

"Here it is!" he was thinking. "Here is the eternity of life preserved for millennia to come..."

"I bought it from a sailor," the sculptor said. "It is a fragment of an ancient people's art, destroyed by barbarians..."

"You see," the Prince muttered at last, "what withstands time is crushed by barbarians. What is art worth if it cannot stop the hand of destruction? Even if it can recreate the intransient in man, it is but a fragile reflection. Alas, I cannot find in it the perfection of Eternity."

The Prince left the studio, his head lowered. A swarthy young man caught up with him. It was one of the sculptor's apprentices, the one who had been singing.

"Please wait!" he cried out. "Not far from here destruction threatens my people, suffering under barbarian rule. Our temples are in ruins or burnt to ashes, people have forgotten our ancestors' legacy, their horses' flying manes and the sound of their swords in battle. I heard what you said. You were speaking the truth. You sight is clear, and your arm is strong. It can wield a sword and bring freedom. I have many friends here. Lead us against the barbarians, for there is no greater glory than the glory of a liberator!"

"A nation is mature enough to be free when it finds freedom within," the Prince replied. "Mine is a different quest, and it cannot be pursued with a sword. Your voice, however, has a magic power to it. Make it a freedom bell. Go to your people and if you manage to awaken them, they will know what to do. Take my horse and my sword, and may God be with you."

The young man's eyes brightened up. He kneeled and kissed the sword, then jumped on the horse and galloped away with a triumphant cry...

twenty

The Prince walked to the piers, found a ship that was about to set off on a long journey, and sailed away. The shore soon disappeared in the distance. The Prince spread his cloak on the deck and lay down.

Moonlit clouds were floating high in the sky, pale stars shining amid them. They looked so distant and unreachable. His mind went back to his questions: "Are mortal men banished from the realm of Eternity? Could the priest be right in saying that the search for knowledge was the original sin? Or are these just legends?"

The Prince held his breath, gazing at the sky.

He had the feeling that it was not the clouds but the stars that were moving... Slowly, majestically, like ships that some giant hand had hurled across space and time...

"What are they? Where are they going? Do they bode glory or ruin? If that is the road to Eternity, is it not for those equal to God, unattainable for mortals?" the Prince mused.

The distant stars were floating silently, offering no answer...

"Will I ever find the way... I wish I could find it out at least in my sleep..."

twenty one

The Prince drifted off to sleep.

In his dream he saw clear deep water in which two fish were swimming slowly, gracefully, as if dancing...

"What could be the meaning of that dream," the Prince mused as he woke up. "Could it be related to the question I have been fretting over?"

It was dawn.

The ship was heading south and the sea was becoming brighter blue.

Dolphins were playing before the prow.

Several weeks had passed when a tall cliff appeared on the horizon, obscure at first, then closer and clearer.

Birds could now be seen in the sky. They seemed to come from the very center of the sun, arcing down before the ship, all the way to the water, their spread wings barely touching it like lips kissing the sea. Then they soared back up and melted into the light...

Slowly, the ship was approaching the cliff. Everyone on board was staring at it. A town could now be seen beneath it. It looked large and prosperous. There was a surge of excitement. They had arrived at their destination.

The pier met them with noise and shouts. Ships were being loaded and unloaded, fish and fruit merchants were praising their ware, buyers were bargaining.

The Prince passed the colourful crowd and headed towards the town centre through a maze of narrow winding streets. Shops on both sides were full of merchandise, their owners inviting passers-by to come in.

The streets smelled of coffee and spices, of dry fish and fragrances. Expensive

twenty two

fabrics, tapestries and carpets caught the eye with their bright colours and ex-
quisite workmanship.

In the goldsmiths' shops, the artisans were creating sophisticated patterns of
gold thread on dark metal utensils with a matte finish, and fine jewels of gold,
gems, pearls, mother-of-pearl and ivory glittered in the displays.

Deeper and deeper into the town's maze went the Prince. He left the noise behind, and in a dead-end street he suddenly found himself in front of the
closed gate of a massive stone house. He was not the kind of man who would
be discouraged by a closed gate.

He turned the handle. The door was not locked. The Prince stepped inside.

He found himself in a courtyard overflowing with flowers and greenery.
A central fountain was spraying its refreshing mist. An old man with a noble
posture and a high forehead was sitting in an antique chair. Surrounded by
scrolls and books, he seemed to be absorbed in thought and did not notice the
newcomer.

"That's it!" he exclaimed suddenly. "Science has the answer!"

"Does it have the answer to the mystery of life?" the Prince asked.

The old man did not look surprised to see him. He replied, as if to himself:

"Perhaps you will help me find that out. I have spent years in studies and experiments, and I have discovered much. But my strength is waning and I need
an assistant. I will share my knowledge with you, although I am still far from
the goal."

"I would love to if you would let me," the Prince replied modestly.

And so he stayed.

twenty three

twenty four

The old scholar was closely studying everything in the world: from the minerals of the earth to the firmament and the characteristics of light, from ancient fossils to living creatures and plants. His library contained remarkable books and manuscripts. Immersed in them, the Prince did not even notice how the days passed.

The Prince and the old scholar expanded what they knew and explored new frontiers of knowledge. They would perform intricate experiments to see how substances interacted. They would polish crystal prisms and watch the white sunlight pass through them and form a fan of strips in all colours of the rainbow. They would make lenses to increase the magnifying power of their telescope. On clear nights they would go up to the highest terrace, observe the sky and draw celestial maps.

Sometimes ships' captains would visit them to order navigation tools and discuss their plans.

To uncover the secret of life, the scholar and his disciple sought to understand in detail the inner workings of all living things.

Once, as they were observing a bird's entrails, the old scholar spoke quietly:

"The human body is no different from an animal's body. We already know much about the functions of its constituent elements, but my lancet has never discovered the organ where the soul resides. I've been wondering, could man be just another, more sophisticated animal?"

"We may not have it all," the Prince replied, "but our knowledge will be of use to people. Wouldn't it be better to share it with them?"

twenty five

"My friend, I once knew a scholar who thought along the same lines. He was burned at the stake as a heretic. This country is not the place, and it is not the time for such revelations. We need to survive so that we can carry on..."

One day, as they were sitting by the fountain in the courtyard, the old man picked up an autumn leaf from the ground, gazed at it and said:

"The small object resembles the large one. The leaf reflects the structure of the tree. There is a law of similarity encompassing all creation. Assuming that it is a game of blind coincidence is like placing a pen in an ape's hand, expecting it to write something meaningful. If I could only touch the Creator's thought!"

The Prince and the old scholar constructed flying models that looked like birds. They tried to build a flying device that would be capable of carrying a man on its wings.

The Prince was so carried away that increasingly often he would look for answers even in his sleep. Indeed, he had a dream about a bird made of light. Like a seagull, it soared high in the dark sky, its wings not moving at all.

Sometimes the Prince had dreams of himself flying above valleys and hills with just an effortless movement of his hands. In his dream, it was clear that although he was flying so high, he would be safe as long as he felt no fear.

"Indeed," the Prince thought, "fear attracts like a magnet the very things that you fear."

A year passed. But the deeper the two delved into the hidden recesses of knowledge, the more questions arose.

One day the Prince heard the old man whisper to himself, gazing into the telescope: "Ah, that eternal silence of boundless space... No, it's not there... The answer is not there..."

twenty six

Sometimes the Prince himself felt discouraged. Each new piece of knowledge seemed to expand the realm of the unknown, often causing them to revise their conclusions. He would then realise that a lifetime would not be enough to get the full answers to at least some of the many questions that filled his mind and inspired his imagination.

One night, the Prince had a strange dream. An open book was in his lap, and he could see clearly the images and the text of the pages he had already read. The unread ones were transparent – there was nothing on them. However, as he looked at them from a different, unusual angle, they were suddenly full of clear images and text. In his dream, he was aware that this information was of crucial importance.

Surprised by the realisation that certain things were inaccessible from the usual viewing angle, the Prince woke up. He tried to go back to sleep, hoping to see some more, but the dream was gone.

"Something is missing in our research," the Prince mused. "Could it indeed be that the most essential is invisible to the eye, and that a different approach is required? And what sort of approach would that be?"

After two years of efforts the old scholar quietly passed away, as if still pondering over the secret to which he had devoted his life.

Without warning, sombre-faced men in dark clothes burst into the large old house, rummaged through the books and manuscripts and found them contradictory to the dogmas they had established.

They burned the old scholar's body at the stake and sent their guards after the Prince, but they were too late. Alerted by the old scholar's loyal friends, the Prince had managed to get away and go into hiding. On a moonless night, he boarded a foreign bark and set sail for an unknown destination.

twenty seven

twenty eight

This time, fate was less kind to the Prince. It was as if he was pursued by the same dark force that had denounced so much hard-gained knowledge and sent books, heretics and witches to the stake.

They were approaching land when a storm hit and the bark ran into a reef and sank. The Prince held on to a wooden plank and survived. At dawn the distant outline of a shore came into view, and he swam towards it. After some time he realised that he was not moving forward. The rolling waves were creating the illusion that they were pushing him towards the shore while the invisible current of a groundswell pulled him back.

"The only way to fight something that is stronger than you is by pretending to yield to it," the Prince remembered the old scholar saying. "Do not struggle with the waves, follow the water, become one with it!"

He changed direction and swam along the shore. Instantly, the water's resistance diminished and the shore slowly drew closer. Exhausted and hardly able to breath, the Prince finally felt the sea floor under his feet. A wave washed him ashore and he passed out...

He was found unconscious by people from the local tribe. They lived in wattle huts plastered with clay. Their bodies were slender and looked as if they were carved of ebony. They were hunters and made fire using dry sticks and tinder.

The Prince gave the shaman a magnifying glass that had somehow survived intact and taught him how to light a fire using the rays of the sun.

twenty nine

The dark-skinned people observed the Prince with curiosity. His friendliness and his many skills won their confidence, and they gradually accepted him as one of their own.

The Prince also had much to learn from these hardy people who knew how to survive in the harshest conditions. Instead of struggling against nature and against all hardships, they seemed to be as free and flexible as reed, at one with life.

Soon came a time of drought, and the herds had to move to more fertile land. The tribe abandoned their homes and followed the cattle.

They crossed desert plains and hills, strewn with the carcasses of animals who had died of hunger and thirst, or had fallen prey to predators.

They had wandered for what seemed to be ages before the first raindrops tapped the dust, announcing the onset of torrential rains.

Suddenly the dry riverbeds were flooded, fresh grass grew rank in the savannah, and the seemingly lifeless trees turned green.

It was so humid that it was hard to breathe. To the beat of tam-tams, the shaman murmured incantations, performed healing rituals and protected the tribe from mysterious evil forces. He was probably good at it, for his primitive methods and strange rituals seemed to yield results.

The Prince was amazed that such forces actually existed and that their action could be felt.

One night, he saw flames in the vapors over the marsh.

"The spirits," the shaman whispered.

"Marsh gas," the Prince replied.

"That's what they seem to you, but you need to have a closer look."

thirty

The shaman was smoking his bone pipe, his eyes half-closed.

"I would like to see them."

"Are you sure?" The shaman turned his half-closed eyes and stared at the Prince.

"What can I learn from them? Do they know the secret of life?" the Prince asked incredulously.

"They know more than you do," shrugged the shaman. "You have to drink some of this potion to be able to see them."

The Prince hesitated for a moment, but he trusted the shaman. His herbs and potions had restored him to health after the shipwreck. He took a sip. His body soon went limp, and he thought he was losing consciousness...

When he came to, the Prince saw the shaman, still smoking his pipe imperturbably.

"Well," he spoke, "did you ask your questions?"

"Disgusting creatures! Was it a dream? They said they were masters of the earth and they had created everything under the sun."

"They like to see it that way. Indeed, they are among the forces that build the visible things. But they are not the creators." The shaman drew on his pipe and went on. "The bow's string sends the arrow flying but it is the archer who pulls the string."

"They promised me power over the forces of life," the Prince went on. "But I have to do as they say."

The shaman smiled.

"They would really be happy if you worship them as gods. What is your decision?"

thirty one

"I don't trust them. My heart is telling me that even if I gain certain skills, I will lose much more. I don't think I should get involved with them."

The shaman gave him a penetrating look.

"There is light within you, and you can feel it. You only need to awaken it."

"How can I do that?"

"Even if I told you now, you wouldn't understand. When a seed sprouts, it will show above the ground. A wise man never picks the fruit before it's ripe. Listen to your inner voice..."

The shaman stood up and walked away. Alone in the dark, the Prince was left to ponder over his enigmatic words. Suddenly, two small round flames appeared, glittering on the branch of a nearby tree. Then there were three flames. The Prince looked more closely and the weak light of the dying fire revealed a troll. It looked as if it had just come out of a fairy tale. His eyes were glowing in the dark. Just like the shaman, it had a bone pipe in its hand. The dwarf giggled and shook its head.

The Prince shouted and lashed at it. He heard a piercing shriek, and the troll was gone.

Still shocked and confused, the Prince wondered whether he had seen a troll or a bird. Could it be that he had not yet recovered completely from his half-sleep?

"Whatever it was, I'll never again try anything that even temporarily deprives me of my free will," the Prince resolved. "It is only to a clear and sober mind that truth can be revealed."

A year later the tribe returned to the same place by the sea. A life circle had closed. However, it was nothing like the swallow's song in the palace park.

thirty two

Often, lying in ambush with the hunters, the Prince would witness bloody scenes of predators chasing their prey.

"How mercilessly each living thing asserts its right to live," he thought as he watched a lioness devour an antelope. The antelope was not dead yet, it raised its head weakly to look helplessly at the beast. "The victim's suffering matters nothing, it is just a piece of meat... As if the one life force has passed through a prism and has been broken into countless multi-coloured lines... Each struggles for survival with the naivety of a beast, but there is no malice in their cruelty. This is why the clash is not destructive, it is part of a whole: of the pulsating circle of life in which all living things matter, complement each other and depend on each other... There is much depth beyond the visible."

Without realising it, the Prince had gradually begun to feel he was an integral part of it all, too, like the people of the tribe.

thirty three

thirty four

Early one morning, a ship appeared by the shore. The Prince rubbed his eyes. He was not dreaming. Waving his arms, he rushed out to the approaching boat, and helped the sailors replenish their stock of fresh water.

The captain was surprised to recognise in the tanned shipwreck survivor the old scholar's disciple: he had visited the old man more than once to seek advice. Well aware of his skill in using navigation devices, he not only agreed to take him on board but even invited him to join the crew as his assistant.

There was also another reason behind the invitation: the captain did not trust his crew completely and kept the maps and the ship's course to himself.

The ship was sailing to some faraway land.

So calm until recently, the sea was getting rough. High long waves appeared. Even when the weather was clear, the vast expanse of water looked heavy and lead-grey. Flying fish shot out of the waves, their vibrating fins glittering like crystal. After many obstacles and storms, the ship finally reached an emerald-green sea. Broad golden bands of seaweed rocked gently on its surface. Fish were hiding in the shadows, and turtles, startled by the ship's approach, paddled frantically into the deep. At the captain's command, they cast anchor by a long beach covered with silk-white sand. Beyond it impenetrable jungles spread as far as the eye could see.

The sailors headed toward a lone hill in the distance. They had to cut their way through lianas and thick undergrowth, and they advanced slowly. In the

thirty five

dim light, they could hear shrieks, birds singing and disturbed snakes hissing. Monkeys stared at them through the foliage, and huge lizards lurked on the lower branches.

Exhausted and desperate, the men suddenly came across terraced pyramids, long engulfed by the jungle. Throughout their journey, the sailors had dreamed day and night of gold and wealth. Now the thought that they had found it brought greedy sparks to their eyes.

The stone pyramids were covered with blood-freezing images: priests offering human sacrifices to winged gods, blood dripping from their knives and down the black drains running steeply from the altar to the ground.

The men searched the pyramids thoroughly but found no gold.

"Temples to death," the Prince thought. "Those poor people! How much human blood was shed to appease the monsters they worshipped?"

As he stared at the winged images, he remembered the shaman's words: "They want to be worshipped as gods but they are spirits of the abyss; they don't care how many living creatures they will kill."

Not finding a living soul on that shore, they sailed away.

They travelled among tiny islands covered by huge trees with thick glossy leaves. Blocked by the thick mass of entangled mangrove roots, the shores were not good for landing.

After several months of wandering, a mutiny broke out. Angry that the captain had not delivered on his promise of wealth and gold, the sailors killed him and threw his body into the sea.

thirty-six

They were about to kill the Prince, too, but their leader stopped them:

"Wait!" he shouted. "We need him! We're after gold and wealth, and gold and wealth we're going to get! Knights of success, show him our generosity!"

They locked the prisoner in the hold, and brought him out once a day to check the course.

When they were back in familiar waters, they cast anchor by a deserted shore, raised a pirate flag and started feasting and singing.

They brought the Prince out to the deck, and to him their faces looked full of hidden malice. Rum was flowing like water, and the pirates were all drunk. The prisoner managed to hide among the scattered barrels and canvases. Then he slipped quietly down a rope to a safety boat that was rocking gently alongside the ship.

The pirates did not notice his escape until the boat moved away from the ship. They shot at him, and hit the boat. By the time it burst into splinters, the Prince had jumped into the sea.

Hiding behind the rocks near the shore, he saw the pirates sail away, but he stayed there until they were gone.

thirty seven

thirty eight

Brarely the fugitive wandered through the desert but found nothing to eat or drink except salty ocean water. Only then did he realise why the "knights of success" had so readily given up the pursuit and left him to his fate. Without the knowledge he had acquired during his stay with the tribe, he would never have survived.

A few days later, he encountered a caravan. Merchants were taking their goods to the nearest harbour.

As soon as they discovered that the Prince could speak their language, they became particularly friendly, offering him water and food and inviting him to join them.

When they finally reached the harbour, the Prince thanked his saviours and joined another caravan that was travelling inland.

They followed an oasis along a wide yellowish river. Thin-legged heron-like birds with curved beaks like crescents walked amid the riverside reeds, as if absorbed in a search for something lost in the silt. Wild geese, ducks and countless other water birds filled the air with their calls.

It was getting dark as they arrived in a big town. A call for prayer was coming from the minarets.

Dominating the skyline were three giant pyramids and the outline of something like a huge lion with a human head. Towering outside the town on the western bank of the river, they looked magnificent in the sunset. Inexplicably, they created a feeling of peace and serenity.

thirty nine

Amazed and intrigued, the Prince heard from the local people that there were more interesting sites further upstream. The following morning he travelled on. Several days later, he reached the ruins of giant temples. There were tombs cut into the rocks, and drawings and inscriptions of incredible beauty.

The half-buried stone effigies of proud kings exuded the same peace and serenity. The Prince could feel the magnificence of a great civilisation. The people who inhabited the oases by the river, however, were not even aware of it.

Tranquillity and oblivion surrounded the ancient temples.

Instead of cool gardens and the murmur of fountains, there was only the sand of time that the hot wind was blowing from the desert.

At first glance, the art brought to mind nothing but tombs. The Prince, however, noticed that it looked more like preparation for eternal life.

There was a mystery here. Gods of varied appearance held the key to that life, touching the humans before them...

"A key," the Prince mused. "What about our sacred books? Could there be a key to them, too? And who among the mortals would know what that would be, and how to use it?"

Bizarre signs – images of men, animals, fish, birds, reptiles, plants, stars and many other symbols – were engraved in the stone in vertical columns.

The Prince could not decipher the unusual inscriptions, but he could feel in them the same urge to discover the secret of Eternity that was driving him, too.

One of the images caught his eye.

A woman with a slender body, sprinkled with stars, was arched over two other figures, gracefully resting on her fingers and toes. One was a male figure,

forty

lying beneath the arched woman. The other figure was standing, as if keeping the two apart – or, perhaps, on the contrary, connecting them?

This was not difficult for the Prince to interpret: the star-covered woman was the sky, the male figure was the earth, and the figure standing between them was the ocean of air that connected and divided them.

He felt this interpretation to be a bit simplified. These figures had further, deeper meaning.

He continued to stare at the image.

There was something feeble about the lying man, raised on his elbow and gazing at the ground.

The figure in the middle had her cupped hands raised towards the female figure, as if to fill them with something flowing from her. Standing alone but also connected with the lying male figure, she seemed to be his duplicate of a sort, an embodiment of his forces, alert but also separate and unrealized.

forty one

Suddenly, as he was stroking thoughtfully the lines, the Prince had the feeling that he was somehow becoming one with the image. His inner eye could now see clearly, and he grasped how these people perceived the universe.

There were three worlds, adjacent and intertwined.

The upper one was the sublime and eternal Spiritual World, the source of life and light; it was the aim of their drive towards Eternity.

The lower one was the earthly world of man, looking away from the Spiritual World and absorbed in his environment.

In between was a zone bursting with energy, willpower and creativity, dividing but also connecting the two worlds.

"How simply it is all expressed," the Prince exclaimed. "Indeed, these symbols speak clearly to my heart. Something dormant deep inside me is awakening, something I feel I have known before!"

forty two

The Prince had noticed that in many of the images the gods had animal heads.

"It seems that the ancients believed that the divine could only reach the humans and be perceived by them through the bestial," the Prince continued.

"Judging by the features of those images in the ruins, the bronze cast I saw at the sculptor's studio must have come from this land," he thought.

The ancient ruins had had other visitors, too. The Prince found out that the locals had been using stones from the temples in their own buildings. There were also signs of treasure hunters. The Prince found the corpses of two of them in a remote ravine. Dried with time, they lay by the remains of a fire and smoke-blackened pottery fragments. The Prince raked up the fire and found a gold ingot.

"Those wretched creatures probably melted a relic, but in their greed they had a falling out and killed each other," he concluded.

Next the Prince came across a tomb, plundered and devastated. The heavy stone sarcophagus was open, and in it lay a mummy, meticulously prepared for Eternity.

"The cocoon is pierced and the butterfly is gone," the Prince thought. "It seems that the ancient people believed this empty shape could further serve its owner. I can't see what it could be used for. Butterflies never go back to the cocoon... Wouldn't it be wiser, then, to look for my own source, instead of digging up old ones?"

He left the world that was buried in the sand, and travelled on with the caravans.

forty three

forty four

The Prince headed east, in the direction of the regal stone lion's gaze, until he faced a vast wasteland. The caravans tended to avoid it, and would make a long detour that took months. The Prince sought a cameleer guide, but only one agreed to negotiate. Infected and swollen, the guide's left eye was nearly closed.

"Why do you want to go across," he inquired. "Hardly anyone ever goes there. It is a desert within the desert."

"Are you scared?"

"We are children of the sands. We are not scared, our fate is in the hands of the Almighty. I have crossed this area twice. Do you have a reason to want to cross here?"

"This is the direction I need to follow, for I have a goal. I'll pay you handsomely," the Prince replied and showed the Bedouin the gold ingot he had dug up from the ashes. The precious metal was a solid argument, and the cameleer's eyes brightened up. In his mind he could already see the camels he would buy with the money.

The Prince hesitated. "He could kill me in the wilderness and take the gold, risking nothing," he thought. But he immediately rejected the suspicion: he knew that the Bedouins were men of honour. Once they made a commitment to protect someone, they would protect him at the cost of their lives.

forty five

The small caravan of two men and four camels slowly made its way into the sinister barren land. The locals had a name for it, which meant "death is near". There were no seasons there, nor anything else. It was as if the sand-glass of the world had been broken in that god-forsaken land, and time had stopped. The two men didn't even speak, perhaps awed by the silence of the desert – or perhaps because they were afraid that death might hear them?

When the wind blew at all, instead of coolness it brought the heat of an open oven. Sometimes it would sweep the dunes' tops. And the sands would moan. Day after day that moaning drained the Prince's strength.

Everything human seemed to be light years away from Eternity. His heart was losing faith, and despair was setting in.

An overwhelming sadness came over the Prince, for he had found nothing under the sun that might recreate life for Eternity...

Suddenly, as it was moving along, one of the camels collapsed and died.

"That was the oldest one. I have crossed this land with it before," the guide spoke sadly and stared at the remaining camels. Both they and the travellers were completely exhausted.

"There is one last stretch to cover," the cameleer went on, "but we need to find the well."

They failed to find it, though, because of the wind. There was something un-usual about it, and the cameleer's face darkened.

"The simoom is coming," he said. "We have to stop and get ready for it."

The camels kneeled down, bellowing and sniffing the air anxiously. The cameleer and the Prince carefully unloaded and covered them, then cuddled beside them and covered themselves, too. Soon the sky and the sun were drowned in sand. The dunes seemed to move, and darkness fell over the place.

forty six

All they could hear was a loud rumble like the sound of a trumpet, powerful and threatening.

It all ended as suddenly as it had started, as if nothing had happened at all. The landscape, however, was changed. A new dune was rising at the spot where the camels and the two travellers had been lying.

The Prince somehow managed to dig his way out. He felt dizzy and had lost any sense of time. He looked around and saw no one. With a sinking heart, he started digging frantically with his bare hands, looking for the camels and the guide, and despair came over him when he found them dead.

It meant that his time had come, too. There was one last remaining hope: to encounter another caravan looking for the well. As he was checking what had been left of the supplies, something heavy tumbled onto the sand. It was the gold ingot.

"This gold only brings misfortune and death," the Prince cried out in anguish and remorse. "It ought to have stayed buried!"

He walked on under the scorching sun, carrying his meagre supply of food in the saddlebags, and a nearly empty waterskin.

He didn't get far. The last drop of water was gone. Dying of thirst, stumbling along, his feverish eyes beheld the Little Princess.

She had a flower in her hand and tears in her eyes.

"You!" his raw lips whispered. "You are probably bringing all the tears you cried. I'm so thirsty, I can drink every single drop of them..."

The woman was approaching slowly through the haze. She held her hands out and spoke:

"You have suffered enough, my child, but I'll comfort you."

forty seven

forty eight

"That would take stronger hands and quicker feet than you need to catch a jester," the Prince smiled. "We need to catch up with the swallows. Will you help me?"

"You have taken me for someone I am not," the woman replied sadly.

"Who are you then?"

"I'm the one you have been looking for, the only one who can give mortals Eternity," she said. Then she caressed the Prince and kissed him on the forehead.

"Oh, you are not the one I have been looking for," he protested. "You are unable to give me what I want. Your lips are cold, and the lips are the ambassadors of the heart. You may well bring peace and oblivion, but I now know that what I am looking for is Love... Love is giving without asking anything in return... In the name of Love, give me some time, please give me time...," he whispered weakly and passed out.

The woman stared at him. In a fraction of a moment the last grain of sand in the sand-clock of his life would drop into Eternity...

forty nine

fifty

A sudden excruciating pain shot through the heart of the old queen.

"Something awful is happening to our son," she said, a dark flame glowing in her eyes. Those eyes were dry, though... They say that tears are alien to those experiencing profound grief.

The king and the queen never heard from their beloved son again. They broke down in mourning.

After the death of the old king, the queen retreated into a remote monastery and spent the rest of her life there.

The nobles had no time for mourning. They decided unanimously that the Prince had wasted his abilities and talents in the pursuit of illusions, and had done nothing useful for the state. He was soon forgotten: power only befriends outward success.

As for the Little Princess, the nobles did not even remember her – nobles are usually very busy people!

Sumptuous feasts marked the crowning of the Prince's younger brother, and his marriage to the wealthiest princess.

The new king was a tyrant.

And the court changed. The sages were banished. Gossipers became so numerous at the palace, and so involved in a web of slander and scheming, that quiet hissing could be heard in every corner.

The young king liked to contemplate his reflection; pompous halls were equipped with mirrors for him, and in them he could see his wealth double.

fifty one

Cunningly, they even put up mirrors on the opposite walls, and the pomp of the halls glared in endless reflections.

The king could see his reflection in the mirrors, in his children's eyes, and in countless huge paintings and sculptures. Court poets sang praises to him in exuberant odes.

"They were inspired by you, Your Majesty," the rhymesters fawned. "We could as well say that you created them. Your appreciation is to us sufficient reward."

Out of vanity and thirst for glory the king threw his subjects into a series of wars, all invariably described as immensely successful. The people were exhausted in the pursuit of false ideals; they were impoverished and disheartened.

Despite his military "victories" the new king failed to protect the kingdom's integrity, and the kingdom shrunk dramatically in size.

The museums, however, displayed the king's images: on horseback, or holding a sceptre, showing off his magnificent garments.

Thanks to art, in many people's eyes he was close to Eternity, petty as his "greatness" was...

The Little Princess did not believe that her Prince was dead.

To avoid the new king's attentions, she quietly left the palace and retreated into a small village in the deepest recesses of the distant mountains.

In her heart, she knew that the Prince cherished a passionate dream that could not be measured by the notion of "success" or "failure".

To men like him, death did not mean perdition.

fifty two

The Little Princess could feel his presence everywhere: in the swallows' songs, the stillness of the water, in the gentle touch of the wind coming from far, far away...

And the pain did not break her spirit, for those who live not for themselves but in Love will live forever...

fifty three

Chapter two

Jesus answered her, "If you knew the gift of God and who
it is that asks you for a drink, you would have asked him
and he would have given you living water."
"Sir," the woman said, "you have nothing to draw up
the water with and the well is deep. Where can you get this
living water?"...
Jesus answered, "Everyone who drinks this water will be
thirsty again, but whoever drinks the water I give him
will never thirst. Indeed, the water I give him will become
in him a spring of water welling up to eternal life."

JOHN 4:10,11,13,14.

fifty six

As it happened, the Little Princess was right. The Prince was not dead.

Bending over him, the woman finally spoke:

"I understand. You desire something in the name of someone who is more powerful than I am." She looked away from the ruby heart on the Prince's chest that seemed to be blinding her. Then she stared at something in the distance. A caravan was approaching slowly.

"So be it," Death whispered disappointedly and melted away in the haze, just as she had appeared.

When he finally came to, the Prince found himself lying on the sea shore, under the shadow of a rug. A few small black goats were staring at him with amber eyes; a camel was ruminating. Beyond it was a rocky shore and sparse thorny grass. Beyond that, in the distance, the huge disk of the sun glowed over a string of orange-coloured dunes.

Both the sky and the sea were burning in the heat of the orange sunset.

Bareheaded, the owner of the humble household was standing on a thread-bare rug, his arms relaxed.

He seemed to be praying, and his posture expressed gratitude and faith.

"He prays standing, his face turned to the east," the Prince noted.

The man finally finished his prayer, came up and, seeing that the Prince was awake, he placed in front of him a bowl of milk and a handful of dates.

fifty seven

"Peace be unto you. God bless you, stranger. To a solitary Bedouin, a guest is a gift of God."

As the Prince was eating to regain strength, his host made a fire and boiled coffee. He then invited the Prince to join him.

"A caravan brought you here," he said. "How did you get to this land? Where do you come from, and what news do you have?"

The Prince told him his story.

The old Bedouin was listening intently, without interrupting. By the time the visitor finished his story, the embers were smouldering beneath soft ashes.

The host was quiet for a while, then he spoke:

"Son, you come from a world where the things that surround you are more plentiful than the stars in the sky. There, time is not something that you own but something that chases you.

Everywhere, there are calls, glitter and illusion, like a mirage in the desert. I understand how hard it is to find the right way amidst thousands of directions and desires.

I can see, though, that sensitivity has awakened in your heart, and that you have been pursuing a noble goal. You were brought here by divine providence.

Have you ever contemplated the desert? I thank God every day for having allowed me to marvel its richness. Is there anything deeper than its silence? The desert will teach you to hear the unspoken, to see the shapeless, and to understand what cannot be expressed in words or attained by thought. At first glance there is nothing much here, but everything here is true."

The old Bedouin thought briefly, then he added:

fifty eight

"Great truths are simple. Only in the desert can you realise what water is. There is no greater wealth on earth. Water is the mother of all life. It comprises the silence of the unborn. Water reminds us of the ocean of forces of proto-being, the source of all existence. Is there a greater miracle than being here? And how many people are aware of that and breathe consciously? How many people actually realise that this earthly existence is but a fraction of all life?"

He scooped up a handful of sand and let is slowly trickle from his palm.

"Isn't this the duration of earthly life? It lies at your feet, your time. Each grain of sand is a moment, and each reminds you that you should live every moment. Not in the past, nor in the future. Earthly life is a rosary of moments. If you lose a moment, you lose your life.

Eternity is a Moment. There is no yesterday or tomorrow.

You can waste the moment by not appreciating it, or by not knowing how to make it meaningful. You need a big goal and the right direction..."

The Prince's host went quiet.

The night was deep and pitch-dark. The Prince looked up at the sky and was dumbstruck: he had never seen the stars looking so huge and so close. He had the peculiar feeling that he had become one of them...

"You have studied the night sky," the old man spoke again. "You are used to searching the constellations and the directions. Most people, however, being blinded by man-made candelabra, almost never notice the celestial ones.

When you are in the desert at night, all you can see above are the stars and the Milky Way. The silence is so profound that if you have not been deafened by the sounds of this earth, you will be able to hear the anthem of Creation. Just keep quiet and listen. Listen..."

fifty nine

sixty

The Bedouin stirred up the embers and added more dry twigs. Small bluish flames flickered, licked the twigs and they flared up.

"The fire that brings you warmth in the cold desert night speaks the language of the greatest force there is: Love," the old man went on. "Love, which means giving without expecting anything in return. It is to Love that you owe your survival, and only Love will give you wings. To burn in its eternal Light, or to perish and turn into dust, these are the two options for every mortal's life."

The old man spoke with a quiet but keen voice. His words were like a revelation to the Prince.

"In the desert sun you can see the power of that Light: if you look at it, it will burn your eyes to ashes. No mortal has ever seen God, or could show Him to anyone.

Look at the Moon, however. There you can see the tenderness of Light. It invites you to look deep into yourself. It is not in the realm of the stars, it is in your soul that you can discover the Divine Presence – not as a thought, not as a fantastic vision but as streaming joy and as bright anticipation.

The human body is the most sacred of all temples, for it is the abode of the human soul.

God does not dwell in man-made temples..."

A gentle wind moved the air and caressed their faces. The Bedouin raised a finger:

"Feel the wind and you will find out that the invisible things are infinitely more than visible things. If you can keep your thoughts quiet for a moment you will hear the wind whisper about the invisible presence of the Spirit that is greater than all space.

sixty one

The invisible, however, involves forces that may harm you if you disregard or are unaware of the eternal laws. Be as vigilant as an oryx in the desert. All too often what we call "coincidence" in our chaotic life is the manifestation of forces from the invisible side of the Universe. By the actions will you judge..."

The Bedouin narrowed his eyes, smiled inwardly and went on:

"In a country far away in the north, in the middle of forests and marshes, there lived a virtuous man who had a strong faith in God. In his imagination he saw pictures of heaven, each one more magnificent than the last, but he took no notice of the world around him.

It once happened that he inadvertently got into a bog and started to sink into the mud. He raised his hands in prayer and closed his eyes: "God, I have been so devoted to you. Please deliver me from this misfortune!" The sun was shining on and off through the rushing clouds. The man could feel its warmth on his eyelids, and in his mind he could almost see a descending angel with huge white wings, ethereal like a dream, extending his hand to rescue him...

He had sunk up to his knees in the sticky mud when a chimney-sweeper passed by on his way back from work. He saw the man in the mud and shouted: "Here, catch this rope! Hold on tight and I'll pull you out!" The virtuous man opened an eye, looked at the shabby and sooty chimney-sweeper, and shouted back: "Get away from me, Satan! God will help me!" And he went on praying: "God, you are mightier than any evil force, please deliver me!"

Offended, the chimney-sweeper gathered his rope and walked away.

The virtuous man was up to his chest in the mud when a woodman came down the track, his donkey loaded with brushwood. The woodman scurried about and extended the longest branch to the drowning man: "Here, hold on to it, and I'll pull you out!" The virtuous man opened an eye, cast a glance at the anxious woodman, and replied: "Go your way, don't intervene in my prayers! God will send angels to rescue me!"

In the end, he drowned in the bog.

That's when the archangel appeared.

"I prayed to you so fervently," the man complained. "Why did you let me die?"

"There is a barrier between our world and the visible world. I cannot cross it if I am not in a human body. That's why I sent two people to rescue you but you refused their help. Now all I can do is take you away..."

Aware that his host was not the ordinary Bedouin he had said he was, the Prince listened in silence. "This man is a real sage," he thought, awed. "I'll share with him all my concerns..."

And he stayed with his kind host until he recovered completely.

sixty three

sixty four

Come morning, the sea was the colour of emerald, dark blue in the distance and bright green at the shore. It spread lazily its frothy silk blanket over the beach, moaning softly like a young mother who has finally given birth after a night of pain and expectation.

Pearl-oyster fragments glittered in the coral-coloured sand like countless stars.

The Prince would help his host on his small desert farm, or would walk along the beach, absorbed in thought.

In the evenings the sun plunged its tired blazing face into the sea, and the best and coolest hours of the day were spent in conversation by the fire.

"You have it right," the old man said. "You can discover the secret of life through knowledge. If you fail to, you will be a mere grain of sand, blown about by winds to the end of your days under the sun. Ancient people believed that ignorance was a sin."

"Why do the priests call the aspiration for knowledge the original sin?" the Prince asked.

"The scriptures were written for people who knew the secret of life. In them, it is only hinted at in fables, so that even if they read them, the uninitiated would not understand."

Holding his breath, the Prince waited for him to go on but the old man went quiet.

"The secret of life? Was man indeed exiled from the Spiritual World?"

"That fable is the story of the Spiritual Man's fall into the deepest abyss of

sixty five

the Universe where life is still possible: the Visible World. The reason was that man broke away from God and thus lost his greatest power. Like a falling star, on his own, afraid of the wild forces of Chaos, he accepted the animal body of an earthly creature.

Man's original sin is fear. As man became an earthly creature, he lost his awareness of his spiritual origin and fell prisoner to the dark forces of the Night. This is what happened to all men who dwelled in visible bodies..."

A twig cracked, sending sparks flying, and the Bedouin gazed at the fire.

The only sound in the darkness was the camel's calm rumination, as rhythmical as a ticking clock.

The Prince was the first to break the silence.

"There is too much cruelty and suffering in this world..."

"There is no perfection in the Visible World. It is like looking for the beauty of a flower in its roots in the mud. Without the roots, however, there would be no slender stem, nor a fragrant bloom.

However, man was not abandoned by Eternal Love. Its envoys, the Sons of Light, work silently and secretly, and only seldom do they reveal themselves to humans. Their noblest goal is to illuminate – in the darkness of lost spirituality – the way of the fallen to their true home. This way, however, is unlike the roads of the earth; it is within you, and only the wings of Love can carry you along it..."

"Can you find the Kingdom of God in your lifetime?"

"You can't find anything you don't believe in.

Search as you did before, but this time within. Not in the bodily organs, for they too belong to the outer world. The soul of the immortal Divine Spark

sixty six

every man unknowingly possesses does not belong in this world. You can attain it, however, even in your lifetime, in a magical way, provided that you find the key..."

At the word "key" the Prince became even more attentive.

"You have to go deep into your innermost nature."

"What does that mean? What is one's innermost nature?"

"You still believe that your thoughts and your body's characteristics are the deepest things in you, your soul," the old man smiled. "However, even if they were touched by Eternity, they are but your outer self. If you want to find the key, you have to look where it resides – beyond the noisy scuffle in the bog of thoughts and earthly desires, beyond the darkness of your closed eyes, where you are alive in each and every one of your cells..."

"How can I do that?"

"The right attitude will suffice. Keep your spirit calm and serene, like the colossi you saw by the pyramids.

Those who torture their "sinful flesh" seeking spirituality are very far from the Spirit: each tiny cell of this mortal body is an altar to a spiritual power. It is the most valuable tool you possess here on earth.

Therefore, in quiet moments that you choose, without any effort or tension, all your limbs relaxed, try to be completely silent. When you arrive at the subtle border between wake and sleep, where thoughts are drowsing but your awareness is there, focus your relaxed mind on the idea and the feeling that your entire body is a clay pot of life-giving water.

Feel the water filling you, taking the shape of your body. Become aware of its spiritual presence, of it being your essence, the ultimate immersion in the moment. This state of consciousness is a great achievement: it is *the key*. Even

sixty seven

if it is all you acquire, it will suffice, for it will prepare you for the awakening of your deep inner spiritual senses. It is the sound foundation on which rests the heavenly ladder leading to the Living Light. You cannot go any further on your own, however.

Ask that the notion of Life-giving Water that fills you and your will become one with the Eternal Will, inseparable from it, illuminated by Its Light. Without Its help you will never be able to unite your spiritual forces. They are forces of Proto-Being, and each of them seeks to assert itself alone. You have to become their master, not their slave.

Ask for that not as a pauper, but with faith and reverence.

Knock on that door, and you will be found. It is narrower than a needle's eye. Few are those who become small enough to pass through it and grow. Beyond it you will find what you had been given from the start: your Self, the way you were in the Light.

Your knocks on that door are your deeds inspired by Love."

"Master," spoke the Prince, deeply moved. "I wonder how these things you expressed so clearly previously looked to me so impenetrable or even contradictory."

"Do not call me Master. There is but one Master within us. I can only show you from without what you need to build yourself within."

The Prince was thoughtful.

"If God doesn't dwell in man-erected temples, why do men build any?"

The old man smiled, but instead of answering the question, he said:

"There is a fable about the ruler who was about to depart to a distant land. Before leaving, he gave each of his servants various quantities of money, depending on their abilities. He told them to use the money in trade.

sixty eight

When he came back he summoned the servants to see how they had fared."

"I remember," the Prince intervened. "Those who had invested the money in trade doubled it, but the last servant, afraid of losing the single coin he had received, had buried it. Upon his return the ruler rewarded the loyal servants, and reproached the coward for not putting his money in the bank where it would have at least gained interest. The ruler ordered that the coin be taken from that servant and given the most enterprising one who had gained the most. Whoever has, to him more shall be given; and whoever does not have, even what he thinks he has shall be taken away from him."

"What is the meaning of this fable?" the old man asked.

"It is not about money but about man's Heavenly Soul. Whoever succeeds in multiplying it through worthy deeds, he alone shall keep it."

"The light within you put these words into your mouth, my son. Man-erected temples are prayer houses, similarly to the amulet that you wear on your chest: it is charged with the power of love, faith and many people's hope. It is the "bank" where the pious puts the "talent" that has been given to him for safekeeping.

It is not in your power to determine the time and the way that the divine gate will open. However, if you follow the Way of spirit and truth you will yourself be the vessel over which the Divine Spark – your innermost self – will glow. Only through it, in your own way and form, can you reach the Living God.

Only then will you understand truly what intrancient life means, for outside God there is nothing but decay.

Sages say that the efforts of mortals to understand God from without are like the attempts of blind men to imagine an elephant: one touches its trunk and says, it is like a pipe; another touches its leg and says, it is like a pillar; still another touches its ear and says, it is like a fan...

sixty nine

seventy

No one can comprehend the Infinite from without... "

The Bedouin closed his eyes. In the light of the fire, the wrinkles on his face looked as if they had been carved with a chisel.

"Forgive me," the Prince began, "but I would like to ask you one more question. I can see that you are familiar not only with our spiritual teaching, but with other teachings as well. To which caravan do you belong?"

"I follow the caravan of Eternal Love. To the true believer, this makes no difference. Remember: "Love each other as I have loved you."

Besides, no one teaching contains everything: so many things have been added to the sacred books through the ages, often with the best of intentions!

Even today, however, your heart can find the grains of truth in these writing, and this truth will be yours alone..."

seventy one

seventy two

Thus the days went by. Sometimes skinny, emaciated pearl divers would stop by in their boats. They ate only figs and drank only water so that they could endure longer in the deep without air.

One morning a low-leaning triangular sail like a swan appeared in the distance. It was so huge that the boat beneath it could hardly be seen.

The merchants cast anchor by the shore. They were taking a precious load of pearls to some land of wealthy rulers and great sages.

"Go with them, son," the Bedouin nodded. "You will see much, and you may even encounter an old teacher of mine."

"How will I recognise him?" the Prince asked.

"You need not look for him. If you are on the right track, and if he can reveal himself to you, he will find you."

The merchants filled their waterskins from the old Bedouin's well. Intrigued by their stories, the Prince took the Bedouin's advice.

At parting, the old man embraced him, and held him tight as if to give him a fraction of himself.

"Be blessed, son!"

"Will I ever see you again?"

"I believe we'll meet. Some time, in the Eternal Day."

Tail winds drove the boat forward like wings.

seventy three

It crossed a strait between steep cliffs shrouded by fogs, and sailed into a sea that was glittering like a mirror under the tropical sun.

They arrived in a wonderful and hospitable land.

Palms framed fine-sand beaches. Their trunks, slender and graceful like young women's bodies, leaned in the wind, and their long dark-green leaves waved their welcome to the arriving travellers.

Further inland there were hills covered by a thick jungle bursting with life. Elephants with heavy loads on their backs strode solemnly along the dusty reddish roads.

The settlements were populous, their markets crowded, noisy and overflowing with all sorts of goods, fruit, spices and treats.

Silversmiths sold spiderweb-thin silver sheets that would melt in one's mouth: they claimed the sheets protected from illness. Fire-eaters, snake-charmers and fakirs entertained the crowd with their amazing tricks.

Images of gods and humans adorned the stone temples, and the palaces' magnificence and perfection was breathtaking. However, the fragrance of flowers mingled with the stench of filthy narrow streets, where paupers lived in untold misery.

As he was learning the local people's language, the Prince noticed that they were invariably serene and no one felt underprivileged.

"You should enjoy your lot," they would tell him with a smile.

"The most miserable man is he who is unhappy with what he has," said a pauper who was sweeping a street corner with a broom. This was the place he called home.

seventy four

He told the Prince the tale of the monk who knew how to make gold. He had no need for gold, though, so he decided to give it to a pauper. He went to the wisest man in the land and asked who was the poorest there.

"Give the gold to the king," the wise man replied.

The king heard about it and was furious. He demanded an explanation.

"Am I the poorest man in this land?" he asked.

"Of course you are, Your Majesty," the sage replied. "No matter how much you've got, it's never enough."

The pauper finished the story triumphantly and smiled.

"This is indeed a happy man," the Prince thought.

In the markets one could hear anything from wild absurdities and superstitions to profound wisdom.

Hermits tortured their bodies in search of spirituality.

In the streets all sorts of fakirs displayed to what extent one could control one's body. The Prince would spend hours watching their skills and postures, acquired after years of patient effort.

The fakirs knew amazing tricks. One of them made an iron ring materialise out of thin air, and handed it to the Prince. He rubbed it: the ring was as real as could be.

"Indeed, this man's skills are incredible," the Prince thought. "He controls more than the body's hidden energies. What price is he paying for the obedience of the weavers of the visible world? And who controls whom?"

Several days later the ring vanished into thin air, just like it had appeared.

Both the rich and the poor welcomed the Prince. They fell over themselves to offer him hospitality, and enjoyed the stories about his travels.

seventy five

The rumour about the strange traveller reached the local ruler, and he wished to meet the Prince, so he invited the Prince to join him on a hunt.

"Everything is clear to me when I chase the prey," he said. "When I listen to the sages' teachings about God, I cannot figure out the truth. Each of them says something different."

"A tree has many branches but a single trunk," the Prince replied. "If you want to get to the truth, go towards the roots, not towards the branches."

Later that day, there was a reception at the palace, and many courtiers were invited. Sitting next to his guest, the ruler was wearing an expensive silk turban, a large green emerald pinned above his forehead.

Dancers glided amidst the dizzying fragrances to the beat of ancient instruments.

One of them disturbed the Prince's peace of mind with her beauty and her graceful dancing. Her long eyes were the colour of violets, gold jewels jingled on her wrists and ankles as she moved with the music. It was a dance of love.

The ruler, too, was watching her intently.

"She is the gem of my dancers," he said as he leaned towards the Prince.

The feast came to an end and the Prince retreated to the apartments that had been prepared for him.

"How quickly the night falls," he thought as he listened to the crickets.

A soft clinking forced him out of his dreaminess.

A shadow slipped into the room, and the dancer sat at the edge of the silk-covered bed.

"Why are you here?" the Prince exclaimed.

"By my master's will," she replied.

seventy six

The Prince watched her, unable to conceal his admiration. Her skin was smooth and silky; her shiny black hair fell in a heavy braid.

"What is *your* wish?" he asked quietly.

"My wish can only be my master's wish. Only the art of love is mine."

"Even if I ask you to stay for the night?"

"I will do it. I was chosen tonight as his gift to you." She was quiet for a moment, then she added: "But if I had the right to a wish, I would have chosen to be with him and give him offspring. No one would ever know that it would be him, reborn. Even himself, he would not know."

"So you love him that much?"

"You are a stranger, you don't understand. This is the only way I could keep him."

The Prince stared at her and finally spoke:

"You are wrong. I may be a stranger here, but not in the world of Love. You are free to go. This is my gift to you."

The girl gaped. Then she came up, kissed him on the forehead, and the clinking of her bracelets melted away in the darkness.

Sleep would not come. The Prince could feel himself surrounded by a strange aura. It seemed to exude not from this world but from within him...

Three years passed.

The Prince followed the advice of his desert Master. He sought to live every moment of his life. He sensed the inner barrier separating him from something anticipated but yet unknown grow thinner. Yet he was still unable to break through it.

seventy seven

He had long stopped studying the birds but he still sometimes had dreams of flying, his soul singing: "Love the grass and the woods, the streams, the rivers and the oceans, love every living creature in them, large or small, to the last grain of this earth. It is your home, your shelter in the cold and the dark of end-less space..."

He got to know better the people of that wonderful land.

Watching the sculptures of divinities in the temples, he would compare them with those he had seen by the pyramids, and again the spiritual beings had many different faces, and some images were of animals.

"I can see you enjoy it all," a Brahmin addressed him with a sly smile. "Don't you find this variety confusing?"

"Nothing in this world is what it appears to be," the Prince replied. "Like a di-amond with countless facets, the Divine casts thousands of reflections, but is still one. Doesn't the same apply to the world around us?"

The Brahmin stared at him inquisitively.

"Only a sage can reach this insight," he said. "You cannot give it to anyone else in words. Everyone has to experience it himself. We have a legend about the hermitage of one of our greatest Masters.

Looking for guidance and enlightenment, he spent long years in meditation and seclusion. He called upon God and expected Him to come, but nothing happened.

In despair, he finally headed back to his home town.

"Am I the most wretched of all creatures so that even the Almighty would despise me?" he kept asking himself. As he walked heart-broken, he saw a scabby dog. It was suffering terribly because worms were eating at its neck, and it could not reach them.

seventy eight

Overwhelmed by compassion, the hermit rushed to help. To avoid hurting the worms with his fingers, he suppressed his disgust as he kneeled by the dog and tried to pull them out with his lips. He closed his eyes and bent over the dog but his forehead touched the ground.

He looked up. The Almighty God was standing before him in all his glory.

"I called upon you for so many years, glorious God," the hermit gasped, "and it is only now that you appear?"

"I was with you all the time but you couldn't see me."

Overjoyed, the hermit prayed to the Almighty to go with him, so that the others might also see him. The Almighty agreed and they walked together. His face gleaming, the hermit kept looking about, expecting his fellow men's awe. But no one noticed.

Only the village diviner saw a scabby dog walking beside him...

The Prince travelled far and wide, through forests and hills, and reached the bank of a wide river where stone temples soared and countless pilgrims crowded. He crossed the river's sacred waters and went further north towards the mountains.

At last he came to a land of secluded monasteries and small distant villages.

Monks in orange robes performed festive rituals. They blew long pipe-like instruments which gave a deep call sounding something like "OhhhMm". The Prince could feel its vibration in his chest, and it invariably evoked the same image: the glorious throbbing circle of earthly life in which all things were interconnected and depended on one another. In the Prince's mind, however, that circle was now broader and encompassed an even larger, infinite circle involving the worlds of the Universal Spirit and the Spiritual Forces.

seventy nine

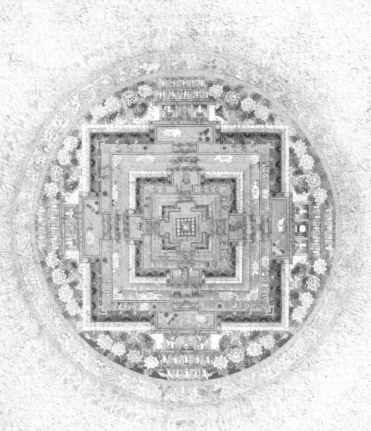

eighty

Between their prayers, the monks would patiently and meticulously draw ornaments in geometric shapes on the pavement, using coloured sand. Squares and circles gradually formed the sand carpet of a mandala. When it was finished, the monks destroyed it and started anew.

"Why did you destroy it," asked the Prince in surprise. "I think it was perfect!"

"External images are transient, like everything under the sun," a monk replied with a calm smile. "It was not important itself; what is important is what is preserved in your soul, the inner image of the mandala as the symbol of the Universe. You must learn to be patient, persevering, concentrated and unattached to ephemeral things. Thus, every worldly activity, no matter how transient or insignificant, if performed with love, will become your teacher."

eighty two

One morning the Prince was walking in the forest at the foot of the monastery where he was staying. There was a strange feeling of emptiness in his chest. "In fact, it cannot be described as emptiness," he thought. "It involves everything, and it is full of energy."

Gentle light shone through the branches, and dew drops glittered on grass blades.

Absorbed in thought, the Prince had walked far away from the monastery. The forest became less and less dense, finally giving way to shrubs and clearings.

A settlement appeared in the distance. The Prince walked on.

He suddenly saw a child in a clearing, not far away from the village. It appeared to be about three years of age.

"A child?" the Prince wondered. "Could it have got lost?"

He then saw a woman carrying a basket.

"Ah, his mother, probably picking herbs..."

The boy stood up and held a dandelion to his pursed lips; he was trying to blow the seeds. A few flew off but some stuck to his mouth and the child removed them angrily with his hand. He kneeled back and tried to pick another dandelion. It turned out to be tough, and the boy pulled at it as hard as he could. Suddenly, the dandelion was uprooted and the boy sat back. The Prince's laughter was cut short at the sight of a tiger in the thickets.

The tiger was stalking the child. It approached slowly and quietly, step by step, his tail beating softly against the earth. The Prince had a dagger in his belt, but, strangely, he didn't think of it.

He took several leaps and got to the child before the tiger. His arm stopped the beast, and he gave a piercing yell. The scream came from each and every fibre of his body.

The beast froze. A couple of seconds passed – to the Prince they felt like eternity – in which they stared at each other. Then the tiger lowered its head and growled, showing its teeth. It didn't move, however. The Prince didn't move, either. The beast looked discouraged. It growled again, this time looking bored. Then it turned around and walked proudly back into the thickets.

The mother was watching the scene in horrified silence, her eyes wide open. Then she rushed towards her child, grabbed him and hurried towards the village. The Prince took the basket she had dropped and followed.

He only caught up with her by the village. The boy, his hand in a fist, was sucking his thumb and staring wide at him from his mother's shoulder.

The woman suddenly stopped and turned to face the Prince.

He was undoubtedly looking at the dancer he had once met. She was as lovely as ever, with a slightly more mature beauty... She recognised him, too.

"How is it that I see you in the most unexpected places," he smiled and looked at the child. "It seems your wish came true. What are you doing here, so far from your ruler's palace?"

The young woman's face went dark for a moment, as if a memory had brought her pain.

The Prince realised he ought to ask no questions.

eighty four

eighty five

"Please," she spoke, "Be my guest! My home is no palace but I own everything in it."

She looked at him openly, the way only women can.

"Thank you for your hospitality. I have stayed too long as it is," the Prince replied.

"You saved the light of my eyes, and therefore me, too. How could I ever pay you back?"

The Prince smiled again.

"I am expected in the country where I come from. I should go."

He extended his hand with the basket.

"God bless you!" shouted the woman as he walked away.

The Prince walked hurriedly to the monastery. He felt alive in each and every cell of his body.

"Everything within me vibrates like a musical instrument," he thought. "It feels like the time when I listened to the old man's song, or when I watched the Little Princess, but so much stronger!... I seem to be the one who should be grateful..."

The Prince's walk through the forest was taking so long that he thought he might have gotten lost. "This is not the same way I came," he realised.

The Prince suddenly found himself in a vast, flower-sprinkled clearing. He could not remember having seen it before. He looked around, and on a sun-bathed hill far away he beheld the monastery walls. Above them, in the distance, glittered a row of inaccessible snow-covered peaks.

eighty six

The clearing was a flat plateau, in the middle of which rose a wide, flat, shrub-covered hill.

The Prince went closer and found himself at the rim of a deep conical crater. The shrubs were in fact the tops of huge trees.

A tiny track covered by decaying leaves led steeply down. The Prince followed it. A silvery lake glittered amidst the greenery.

The Prince walked down to it.

The lake glistened like a diamond in thousands of colours, and the green trees were reflected in crystal-clear waters that quietly washed the brown-reddish rubble of the shore.

Covered by the same rubble, the bottom descended steeply, with no algae or plants in sight.

The place basked in sacred quiet and peace. Not even a bird could be heard. The opposite shore was getting dark...

The Prince gazed at the lake with an awed smile. He recalled the birds that seemed to fly out of the sun. He kneeled down and kissed the water. Then he immersed himself into it, clothes and all.

It was so cold it burned. Several metres into the lake, he could no longer feel the bottom. Even the sound of his splashing, however, seemed to die in that powerful silence.

The Prince returned to the shore.

He kneeled down again, and gazed at the strange lake, with no streams flowing into or out of it, and huge bluish trunks soaring above it like the arches of a cathedral.

eighty seven

eighty eight

He felt an insight that could not be expressed in words: he soaked up the vast silence, the crystal clarity, and was overtaken with serenity and tranquillity.

There were no more questions, no more fighting thoughts. Past, present and future became one endless moment containing everything. It was as if he had glimpsed the heart of Being, as if he was touched by Eternity.

"Here it is, my Source!... The time of my wandering in the outer world is over," the Prince thought. "Now I am the Way."

A moment later he noticed two fishes swimming in the deep light, slowly and gracefully, as if they were dancing.

"I was given the answer to my question about the Way as early as in my dream on that ship: you will see the way when you see the fishes... I didn't understand it then..."

He heard the sound of flowing water behind him, and he turned around. An old man was sitting on a rock on the hill nearby. He was not wearing a monk's robe, but was dressed in ordinary clothes.

His hair, his eyebrows and his long beard were as white as snow. He resembled strongly the singer with the cittern he had encountered at the palace. His face was more sun-tanned, though, and he was not blind at all!

Sitting in front of a cave in the rock, he was pouring water from a clay pot into an alabaster cup. He extended the cup to the Prince.

The Prince could feel that the man was somehow related to his insight, to the serenity and the tranquillity that had filled him. He accepted the silent invitation and walked up to the old man.

"Peace be with you, son," the man said.

"Do you know me?"

"I have been looking forward to your arrival. I have been with you from the beginning of your quest. I accompany all those who search earnestly."

"I never saw you before."

"The time had not arrived yet. I knew you would come and bring the greetings of my old friend in the desert. I can feel what you feel. Your frail body is a musical instrument, and Eternity plays it.

You are the composer of that music. You are the bow, and the head, and the heart, and the music itself. It is all yours, unlike any other music, still it is part of the great anthem of the spheres, one of all and all in one.

Do you wish to go back where you are expected? Do it! In the earthly world of appearances progress often looks like retreat, and the greatest of all victories – Resurrection – looks like death.

You just took the decisive step to Eternity – that turning of the will inward, to your inner Self.

The road into your own Self is endless. I'll always walk with you, even if I am invisible.

The road will go on even after you leave this world. The Universe is deep – deeper than even the most perfect tools can measure, deeper than the greatest believers can imagine...

You will raise many more curtains of ignorance, and you will overcome many more obstacles. Each and every one of them is a step you need to climb – further up into the spheres of the Spirit, until you are reborn in your spiritual body, like the son of a virgin, shining bright as a precious stone. Such are the stones that build the temple of the eternal Giver who is the Word..."

ninety

ninety one

Epilogue

Here the old manuscript ends. I found it, yellowish and faded, by chance as I was rummaging through the dusty shelves of a library. It would make a nice fable, I thought after I read the scattered segments, were it not unfinished...

I tried to find out the Prince's name at least, but to no avail. He was not to be found in the list of rulers for, following his inner voice, he had pursued an unusual goal: the Path to Eternity. He had followed that road steadily, in body and soul, with the boundless enthusiasm of youth.

It doesn't really matter that I never found his name. A name is something transient, like the history of rulers. Much more important is the eternal universal name, but *no one knows that name except the one who receives it...* [*]

Did the Prince go back to his kingdom?

Did he find the Little Princess?

The records of the court's secret service contain the reports of the spies whom the king had sent to find the Little Princess and bring her back. They had found her house but she had disappeared without a trace. She had probably left the country because local people said one day a stranger had knocked at her door and she was never seen again.

---

[*] John, Revelations 2:17.

ninety two

Might that stranger have been the Prince?

The legend says nothing further, and I prefer not to speculate.

One thing is certain: the Prince reached that moment in life when the important could only be seen from a special angle.

The story had nearly slipped out of my mind, but years later I came across some other books, and in the light of what I read in them the story from the old manuscript came alive in my memory, and everything clicked into place like the elements of a mandala.

The result is what I offer you, dear reader.

As the sages say, the more you talk, the less you say. I will now close the pages of the manuscript.

There are no words in the human language that can express the innermost, and even if you find it out, my friend, every person's inner path is different.

Follow your path with faith and confidence. Follow it in Love.

No one's Living God is the same as yours.

ninety three

A message to the lucky few,

who read all the way through this book without thinking: what sort of a fable is this – at times seemingly abstract and scientific, and not even complete! I wouldn't claim this is a fable that fits the rules. Like that swallow, elocution has never been my strong side. They say Kandinsky went in for abstract painting when he chanced upon a painting that was turned upside down (ah, those accidents!). Thus, having lost the supporting point of subject versus object, he realised the inner beauty of colour and shape beyond the essence. One cannot grasp the outer without first understanding the inner.

Instead of making up an end for this story, I dare to quote a piece of advice. It carries the ancient and eternal truth about the path that the Prince ultimately found, and along which one can only move on the wings of Love.

ninety four

A piece of advice

Accept your life
As it is,
Don't think
How different it could have been,
And don't curse any
Of your days!
If you have to endure something –
Do it!
Bless everything
You ever encounter
And blessed you will be!

Bo Yin Ra*

[*] Bo Yin Ra is the spiritual name of the writer and artist Joseph Anton Schneiderfranken. He was born in 1876 in Aschaffenburg, Germany, and lived in Massagno near Lugano until his death in 1943.

Ivan Stanchev

THE PATH TO THYSELF

First edition

English translation Janeta Shinkova
Editor of the English translation Geoffrey Dean
Graphic design Krassimira Despotova
Computer processing Hristina Mladenova

Print DIMITER BLAGOEV PRINTING HOUSE

KIBEA PUBLISHING COMPANY

Sofia 1336, P. O. Box 70
Tel.: 824 10 20; Fax: 925 07 48
www.kibea.net
E-mail: office@kibea.net

SALES DEPARTMENT

19, Iskarsko Chaussee Blvd., Sofia
Tel.: 973 75 37

KIBEA'S BOOKS & HEALTH CENTRE & RESTAURANT

Sofia, Dr G. Valkovich Street 2A

Bookstore: Tel.: 988 01 93
Health Food Restaurant: Tel.: 980 30 67